The Story of a Special Day
Volume 64

March 4

63rd day of the year
(64th in leap years)
302 days remaining
until the end of the year.

by Michael Dobson

Timespinner
Press

Copyright Information

March 4: The Story of a Special Day (Vol. 64) is copyright © and trademarked ™ 2012 by Timespinner Press. All rights reserved. The Timespinner Press logo is trademarked by Timespinner Press.

For more information about the series, about me, or about your special day, please email us at editor@timespinnerpress.com.

Table of Contents

Cover: "Scene at the Signing of the Constitution of the United States," by Howard Chandler Christy

March 4 Quotations

"It is only when we realize that life is taking us nowhere that it begins to have meaning."

> — *P. D. Ouspensky, born March 4, 1878*

"I decided to get a Ph.D. in experimental physics because experimental physicists have their own room in the Institute where they can hang their coat, whereas theoretical physicists have to hang their coat at the entrance."

> — *George Gamow, born March 4, 1904*

"I would do away with the Education, the ... Commerce and -- let's see -- I can't. The third one, I can't. Sorry. Oops."

> — *Governor Rick Perry, born March 4, 1950*

"The books I write because I want to read them, the games because I want to play them, and stories I tell because I find them exciting personally."

> — *Gary Gygax, died March 4, 2008*

Event of the Day

The United States Constitution Takes Effect

The United States Constitution, originally adopted on September 17, 1787, went into effect on March 4, 1789, with the first meeting of the 1st Congress in New York City's Federal Hall. The Constitution superseded the Articles of Confederation, which provided for a loose alliance among sovereign states, with a document that established a more powerful central government.

While it had become clear that the Articles of Confederation were insufficient to meet the needs of the new nation, there was substantial disagreement on what should replace it. In 1787, a convention of state delegates began meeting in Philadelphia. Originally, only two states attended, but eventually twelve states were represented in the debate.

During the ratification vote, some delegates were disappointed with the result. Of the 55 delegates, only 39 signed. Benjamin Franklin said, "There are several parts of this Constitution which I do not at present approve," but voted to accept it "because I expect no better and because I am not sure that it is not the best."

Nine states were needed to ratify the new Constitution, but after an extensive public information effort (now known as the *Federalist Papers),* eventually all 13 states signed on, although in some cases ratification was a narrow thing.

It took the new Congress some time to get itself organized. On April 1, they achieved a quorum and elected officers, and on April 6 they counted the Electoral College ballots, electing George Washington as the first President by unanimous vote.

From the Preamble to the US Constitution

March 4 Holidays and Celebrations

Saint Casimir's Day

Patron saint of Poland and Lithuania, Saint Casimir (October 3, 1458 — March 4, 1484) was a royal prince of the Jagiellon dynasty. Known for his enlightened rule and for his piety, he was canonized in 1522 by Pope Adrian VI.

The anniversary of his death, March 4, is celebrated in both nations. Numerous Roman Catholic churches established by Polish or Lithuanian immigrants are named for him. The *Kaziuko mugė*, an annual folk arts and crafts fair, is held on the Sunday nearest to Saint Casimir's Day in Vilnius, Lithuania, and attracts tens of thousands from Lithuania and from other central European nations.

The 2007 *Kaziuko mugė* fair in Vilnius, Lithuania

Christian Feast Days

Saints commemorated on March 4 include Adrian of Nicomedia, Basinus, Blessed Humbert III of Savoy, Casimir, and Peter of Pappacarbone.

What Happened on March 4?

1493 CE - Columbus Returns to Europe

After his successful voyage to what would become known as the New World, Christopher Columbus set sail for his return trip on January 15, 1493, but fierce storms diverted him from his intended destination of Spain. On March 4, 1493, he arrived in the harbor of Lisbon, Portugal. After meeting with Portuguese monarch João II, he continued to Spain, arriving in Barcelona on March 15 of that year.

1519 CE - Hernán Cortés Reaches Mexico

On March 4, 1519, Spanish *conquistador* Hernán Cortés landed on the coast of the Yucatán peninsula to begin his conquest of the Aztec empire.

1628 CE - Massachusetts Bay Colony Chartered

On March 4, 1519, King Charles I of England issued a royal charter for the Massachusetts Bay Colony, establishing the legal basis for what eventually became Massachusetts.

1681 CE - Pennsylvania Established

On March 4, 1681, the new colony of Pennsylvania established its first colonial government.

1791 CE - Vermont Becomes a State

On March 4, 1791, Vermont, which had previously been the independent Republic of New Connecticut, became the 14th state, the first to enter the Union after the original thirteen colonies.

1797 CE - John Adams Becomes President

In what has been billed as the "first ever peaceful transfer of power between elected leaders in modern times," John Adams was sworn in as President of the United States on March 4, 1797, succeeding George Washington.

1861 CE - The CSA Adopts Its Flag

On March 4, 1861, the Confederate States of America established its first national flag, known as the "Stars and Bars." Based on the U. S. flag, the original design had seven stars, which grew to 13 before the end of the Civil War.

1890 CE - Forth Bridge Opens

The Forth Bridge, the longest single cantilever bridge span in the world (until 1917), stretched over 2,500 meters (8,200 feet) to cross the Firth of Forth, connecting Edinburgh with Fife. It has been nominated as a UNESCO World Heritage Site by the British government.

1917 CE - **First Female Representative**

Montana Republican Jeannette Rankin became the first female member of the US House of Representatives. Elected in 1916, she began her term in office on March 4, 1917. She was elected again in 1941. A lifelong pacifist, she was the only member of Congress who voted against declaring war after the Pearl Harbor attack.

1918 CE - **USS *Cyclops* Disappears in the Bermuda Triangle**

The US Navy collier (bulk cargo ship) *Cyclops* left Barbados for Baltimore, Maryland, on March 4, 1918. The ship carried 306 crew and passengers and carried over 10,000 tons of cargo

— although it was rated as having a maximum capacity of 8,000 tons. The route carried the ship through what became known as the Bermuda Triangle. It was never seen again.

1933 CE - First Female Cabinet Member

Frances Perkins, previously the New York State Commissioner of Labor, was appointed by President Franklin D. Roosevelt as the fourth Secretary of Labor. Taking office on March 4, 1933, she served until 1945. Her many accomplishments include a key role in the establishment of Social Security and the Fair Labor Standards Act.

1943 CE - Battle of the Bismark Sea Ends

The Battle of the Bismark Sea, a critical Navy engagement in the Southwest Pacific Area (SWPA) theater of World War II, lasted from March 2-4, 1943, resulting in a major Japanese defeat. The US lost 13 people, the Japanese at least 2,890.

Who Was Born on March 4?

The abbreviation "O.S." on some dates refers to the fact that the Russian Empire did not switch from the Julian to the Gregorian calendar at the same time as the rest of Europe, and therefore some figures have two dates for their birth or death.

People whose original names are not in the Western alphabet have their native names in the appropriate script shown in parenthesis.

Arts and Letters

Dav Pilkey (March 4, 1966 —)

Children's author and illustrator Dav Pilkey is best known for his *Captain Underpants* book series.

James Ellroy (March 4, 1948 —)

Crime fiction writer James Ellroy has written numerous novels, including the 1987 novel *The Black Dahlia* and 1990's *L.A. Confidential.* The movie adaptation of *L.A. Confidential* was nominated for nine Academy Awards.

Ward Kimball (March 4, 1914 — July 8, 2002)

Disney animator Ward Kimball was one of the "nine old men," as the core senior animators were known. His notable work includes Jiminy Cricket in *Pinocchio,* the crows in *Dumbo,* Lucifer and Bruno from *Cinderella,* and the Academy Award winning short subject *Toot, Whistle, Plunk, and Boom.*

Barbara Newhall Follett (March 4, 1914 — ?)

Child prodigy Barbar Newhall Follett published her first novel at the age of twelve, and her critically acclaimed second novel at the age of fourteen. On December 7, 1939, she walked out of her house with $30 and was never seen again.

P. D. Ouspensky (Пётр Демья́нович Успе́нский) (March 4, 1878 — October 2, 1947)

Esoteric philosopher P. D. Ouspensky was best known for his expositions of the work of George Gurdjieff.

Acting and Film

Patsy Kensit (March 4, 1968 —)

Actress Patsy Kensit is best known for her role as Rika in *Lethal Weapon 2*.

Steven Weber (March 4, 1961 —)

Steven Weber is best known for playing skirt-chasing pilot Brian Hackett in the 1990s television series *Wings*.

Mykelti Williamson (March 4, 1957 —)

Mykelti Williamson came to prominence for his role as Bubba Blue in *Forrest Gump,* and subsequently played major roles in the television series *Boomtown* and the eighth season of *24*.

Patricia Heaton (March 4, 1958 —)

Patricia Heaton won two Emmy Awards for her role on the TV sitcom *Everybody Loves Raymond.*

Catherine O'Hara (March 4, 1954 —)

Second City Television veteran Catherine O'Hara is an Emmy-winning actress who has appeared in a number of movie roles.

Gunnar Hansen (March 4, 1947 —)

Icelandic-born actor Gunnar Hansen is best known for playing Leatherface in 1974's *The Texas Chain Saw Massacre.*

Adrian Lyne (March 4, 1941 —)

Adrian Lyne was nominated for the 1988 Academy Award for Best Director for *Fatal Attraction* and directed the music video for *Flashdance* theme song "Maniac."

Paula Prentiss (March 4, 1938 —)

Paula Prentiss's many movie roles included *Where the Boys Are, The Stepford Wives,* and *What's New, Pussycat?* She was nominated for an Emmy for her groundbreaking television sitcom *He & She.*

Paula Prentiss (left) with husband and
He & She co-star Richard Benjamin

Barbara McNair (March 4, 1934 — February 4, 2007)

Singer and actress Barbara McNair appeared on numerous television variety shows and drama series, as well as in the Elvis Presley movie *Change of Habit* and Sidney Poitier's *They call me MISTER Tibbs!* She was one of the first

African-American women to host her own television variety series, *The Barbara McNair Show,* which ran from 1969 to 1972.

Barbara McNair (left) with Jim Nabors

William Alland (March 4, 1916 — November 11, 1997)

William Alland played reporter Jerry Thompson in 1941's *Citizen Kane* and produced such films as *It Came from Outer Space* and *The Creature from the Black Lagoon.* He won a George Foster Peabody Award for producing the radio drama *Doorway to Life.*

John Garfield (March 4, 1913 — May 21, 1952)

Actor John Garfield was a major star for Warner Brothers. He was blacklisted after refusing to "name names" before the U.S. Congressional House Committee on Un-American Activities (HUAC) during the "Red Scare" of the McCarthy era, which ended his film career.

Pearl White (March 4, 1889 — August 4, 1938)

Silent film star Pearl White is best known for her starring role in 1914's *The Perils of Pauline,* a silent film serial in 20 weekly installments, each ending in a cliffhanger.

Movie poster for *The Perils of Pauline*, starring Pearl White

Business

Frank Wells (March 4, 1932 — April 3, 1994)

Frank Wells was president of the Walt Disney Company from 1984 until his death.

Ed "Big Daddy" Roth's Beatnik Bandit

Ed "Big Daddy" Roth (March 4, 1932 — April 4, 2001)

Custom car designer, builder, and cartoonist Ed "Big Daddy" Roth was a key figure in the hot-rod culture of the late 1950s and 1950s. His cartoon character Rat Fink (an anti-hero version of Mickey Mouse) is his best-known cartoon creation.

Richard DeVos (March 4, 1926 —)

Richard DeVos co-founded Amway and owns the NBA team Orlando Magic.

Harry Helmsley (March 4, 1909 — January 4, 1997)

Real estate magnate Harry Helmsley owned the Empire State Building, the St. Moritz Hotel, and many other properties. He is best known to the public because his wife, Leona Helmsley, dubbed the "Queen of Mean" was convicted in 1989 for tax evasion. Although Harry Helmsley was also indicted, his poor health made him too weak to stand trial.

Charles Walgreen Jr. (March 4, 1906 — February 10, 2007)

Son of the founder of the eponymous Walgreen drugstore chain, Charles Walgreen Jr. took over the company following his father's death, serving as president and chairman from 1939 until 1976.

Avery Fisher (March 4, 1906 — February 26, 1994)

Audio engineer Avery Fisher invented the transistorized amplifier and the first stereo, and made major improvements in AM-FM tuner design. A noted philanthropist, his donation to the New York Philharmonic is memorialized in the Avery Fisher Hall at Lincoln Center.

Magic and Games

Robert Orben (March 4, 1927 —)

Comedy writer for Red Skelton and Jack Paar, Presidential speech writer for Gerald R. Ford, and magician Robert Orben has written numerous gag books and resources for magicians.

John Scarne (March 4, 1903 — July 7, 1985)

Magician John Scarne was best known for his skills in playing card manipulation. An expert on card games, he wrote a number of popular books on the topic.

Charles Goren (March 4, 1901 — April 3, 1991)

World champion bridge player Charles Goren authored numerous best-selling books on bridge strategy.

Theodore Hardeen (March 4, 1876 — June 12, 1945)

Brother of magician Harry Houdini, Theodore Hardeen, an accomplished magician and escape artist in his own right, founded the Magician's Guild.

Harry Houdini (left) and Theodore Hardeen (right)

Music

Evan Dando (March 4, 1967 —)

Musician Evan Dando leads the alternative rock band The Lemonheads and was voted one of the "50 Most Beautiful" by *People* magazine in 1993.

Emilio Estefan (March 4, 1953 —)

Leader of the Latin pop group Miami Sound Machine, Emilio Estefan is the husband of singer Gloria Estefan.

Bobby Womack (March 4, 1944 —)

Recording artist and composer Bobby Womack was inducted into the Rock and Roll Hall of Fame in 2009.

Miriam Makeba (March 4, 1932 — November 10, 2008)

Grammy-winning singer and activist Miriam Makeba (nicknamed Mama Africa) popularized African music in the United States and campaigned against South African apartheid.

Paul Mauriat (March 4, 1925 — November 3, 2006)

French orchestra leader Paul Mauriat topped the US pop charts in 1968 with "Love is Blue."

Antonio Vivaldi (March 4, 1678 — July 28, 1741)

Italian composer Antonio Vivaldi is best known for his violin concertos known as *The Four Seasons*.

1723 cartoon of Antonio Vivaldi, by Pier Leone Ghezzi

Politics and News

François Fillon (March 4, 1954 —)

François Fillon was prime minister of France from 2007 to 2012.

Rick Perry (March 4, 1950 —)

Rick Perry became the 47th governor of Texas in 2000, and ran for the 2012 Republican nomination for President of the United States. His campaign suffered from poor debate performances, most famously his inability to remember the name of one of the three Federal agencies he would abolish.

Lynn Sherr (March 4, 1942 —)

Lynn Sherr is best known as a correspondent for the ABC newsmagazine *20/20*. She won the George Foster Peabody Award in 1994.

Alice Rivlin (March 4, 1931 —)

Economist Alice Rivlin was vice chairman of the Federal Reserve, director of the White House Office of Management and Budget, and director of the Congressional Budget Office.

T. R. M. Howard (March 4, 1908 — May 1, 1976)

Civil rights leader T. R. M. Howard mentored such activists as Medgar Evers and Jesse Jackson, played a major role in the investigation of the murder of Emmett Till, and chaired the National Negro Business League.

Henry the Navigator (March 4, 1394 — November 13, 1460)

Third child of King John I of Portugal, Henry the Navigator played a critical role in the early development of European naval exploration.

Henry the Navigator

Public Figures

Chaz Bono (March 4, 1969 —)

The only child of Sonny Bono and Cher Sarkisian (better known as the pop duo Sonny and Cher), Chaz Bono (born Chastity Bono) is a transgender man active in LGBT causes.

Lindy Chamberlain (March 4, 1948 —)

Australian Lindy Chamberlain was accused and convicted of murdering her nine-week old daughter in 1980, famously claiming a dingo (wild dog) had taken her baby. Her conviction was overturned eight years later based on additional evidence, and she and her then-husband were acquitted of all charges. In 2012, an Australian coroner, after a fourth inquest, ruled that a dingo had indeed caused the baby's death.

Lois W. (March 4, 1891 — October 5, 11988)

Wife of Alcoholics Anonymous co-founder Bill W., Lois W. co-founded Al-Anon, a support group for friends and family of alcoholics. Her real name, Lois Wilson, was revealed following the death of her husband in 1971.

Science and Engineering

George Gamow (March 4, [O.S. February 20] 1904 — August 19, 1968)

Theoretical physicist George Gamow made major contributions to cosmology, and in later life became publicly known as the author of popular books on science, most famously *One, Two, Three...Infinity.*

Malcolm Dole (March 4, 1903 — November 29, 1990)

American chemist Malcolm Dole is known for the Dole Effect, which measures the relative effects of land-based and marine photosynthesis, allowing measurements dating back 130,000 years.

Wilbur R. Franks (March 4, 1901 — January 4, 1986)

Canadian scientist Wilbur Franks invensted the G-suit, which influenced all subsequent pressure suits and spacesuits. He received the Order of the British Empire for "saving the lives of thousands of Allied fighter pilots."

David W. Taylor (March 4, 1864 — July 28, 1940)

Chief Constructor of the Navy, naval architect David W. Taylor is the namesake of the destroyer *David W. Taylor* (DD-551), and of the David Taylor Model Basin at the Naval Surface Warfare Center's Carderock Division.

Sports

Kevin Johnson (March 4, 1966 —)

Former NBA all-star point guard Kevin Johnson was elected mayor of Sacramento, California, in 2008.

Ray "Boom Boom" Mancini (March 4, 1961 —)

Former World Boxing Association lightweight champion Ray Mancini inherited his nickname from his father Lenny "Boom Boom" Mancini, a 1940s top ranked boxer whose career was derailed when he was wounded in World War II.

Buck Baker (March 4, 1919 — April 14, 2002)

Automobile racing driver Buck Baker was inducted into the NASCAR Hall of Fame in 2013.

Margaret Osborne duPont (March 4, 1918 —)

Tennis star Margaret Osborne duPont won 25 Grand Slam titles at the US championships and was the World No. 1 American female tennis player in 1947.

Lefty O'Doul (March 4, 1897 — December 7, 1969)

Baseball pitcher and manager Lefty O'Doul was instrumental in making baseball a popular sport in Japan and was inducted into the Japanese Baseball Hall of Fame in 2002.

Dazzy Vance (March 4, 1891 — February 16, 1961)

Known for his fastball, Charles "Dazzy" Vance" was inducted into the Baseball Hall of Fame in 1955.

Dazzy Vance

Knute Rockne (March 4, 1888 — March 31, 1931)

Notre Dame coach Knute Rockne is considered one of the greatest coaches in college football history and is a member of the College Football Hall of Fame.

Red Murray (March 4, 1884 — December 4, 1958)

Baseball player John J. "Red" Murray was described as "one of the two greatest right fielders in New York Giant history."

Sam Langford (March 4, 1883 — January 12, 1956)

Called the "Greatest Fighter Nobody Knows" by ESPN, and rated #2 by *The Ring's* "100 Greatest Punchers of All Time," the man known as the Boston Bonecrusher was the World Colored Heavyweight Champion, but was kept from competing for the World Championship because of the color bar.

Who Died on March 4?

Acting

Minnie Pearl (October 25, 1912 — March 4, 1996)

Country comedienne Minne Pearl appeared at the Grand Ole Opry for over 50 years and also appeared on the television show *Hee Haw*.

John Candy (October 31, 1950 — March 4, 1994)

Canadian comedian John Candy came to fame as a cast member of the *Second City Television* series, and subsequently appeared in numerous movies, including *Spaceballs, Stripes, Uncle Buck,* and *Planes, Trains, and Automobiles.*

Bert Williams (November 12, 1874 — March 4, 1922)

One of the most popular comedians of the vaudeville era, Bert Williams was the first African-American to take a lead role on the Broadway stage and was the best-selling black recording artist before 1920. He was called "one of the great comedians of the world" by the *New York Dramatic Mirror.*

Arts

Fred Lasswell (July 25, 1916 — March 4, 2001)

American cartoonist Fred Lasswell wrote and illustrated the long-running newspaper strip *Barney Google and Snuffy Smith.*

Art Babbitt (October 8, 1907 — March 4, 1992)

Disney animator Art Babbitt created the character Goofy and worked on numerous classics including 1937's *Snow White and the Seven Dwarves* and 1940's *Fantasia.* He won more than 80 awards in his long career.

Crime

Mendy Weiss (June 11, 1906 — March 4, 1944)

Louis Capone (1896 — March 4, 1944)

Louis Buchalter (February 6, 1897 — March 4, 1944)

Mendy Weiss, Louis Capone (no relation to Chicago crime lord Al Capone), and Louis Buchalter were all members of Murder, Inc., an association of contract killers. All three convicted of murder and executed on the same day, one after the other.

Letters

Gary Gygax (July 27, 1938 — March 4, 2008)

Writer and game designer E. Gary Gygax co-created the role-playing game *Dungeons & Dragons*.

William Carlos Williams (September 17, 1883 — March 4, 1963)

American poet and physician William Carlos Williams won the first National Book Award for Poetry and received a posthumous Pulitzer Prize.

Bror von Blixen-Finecke (July 25, 1886 — March 4, 1946)

Swedish baron, writer, and big-game hunter Bror von Blixen-Finecke was married to Karen Blixen, a writer whose pen name was Isak Dinesen. The film *Out of Africa* is based on their years living in Kenya.

Nikolai Gogol (Никола́й Го́голь) (March 31 [O.S. March 19], 1809 — March 4 [O.S. February 21], 1852)

Ukranian-born Russian dramatist, novelist, and short story writer Nikolai Gogol is best known for his satires of political corruption in the Russian Empire *(The Government Inspector)* and for his historical novella *Taras Bulba.*

Nikolai Gogol

Military and Exploration

General John Schofield (September 29, 1831 — March 4, 1906)

General John Schofield received the Medal of Honor in the Civil War, served as Secretary of War under President Andrew Johnson, as Superintendent of West Point, and as commanding general of the US Army. The Hawaii military installation Schofield Barracks is named for him.

Jesse Chisholm (1806 — March 4, 1868)

Indian trader, guide, and interpreter Jesse Chisholm is the namesake of the Chisholm Trail, used by western ranchers to drive cattle to eastern markets. Although Chisholm built several trading posts along the route, he never drove cattle on the trail named for him.

Commodore Matthew C. Perry (April 10, 1794 — March 4, 1858)

Known as the "father of the steam Navy," Commodore Perry is famous for his role in the opening of Japan to the West in 1854.

Commodore Matthew C. Perry

Public Service

Thomas Eagleton (September 4, 1929 — March 4, 2007)

Missouri senator Thomas Eagleton was briefly the Democratic vice presidential nominee under George McGovern in 1972.

Harry Blackmun (November 12, 1908 — March 4, 1999)

Associate Supreme Court Justice Harry Blackmun is best known as the author of *Roe v. Wade*.

George Foster Peabody (July 27, 1852 — March 4, 1938)

Banker and philanthropist George Foster Peabody is best known today for the George Foster Peabody Awards given for excellence in radio and television (and since the late 1990s for internet content as well).

Alexander H. Stephens (February 11, 1812 — March 4, 1883)

Alexander Stephens was Vice President of the Confederate States of America during the Civil War, a member of the US Congress both before and after the war, and the governor of Georgia. He was nicknamed "the Little Pale Star from Georgia."

Saladin (1137/1138 — March 4, 1193)

Ṣalāḥ ad-Dīn Yūsuf ibn Ayyūb (Arabic: صلاح الدين يوسف بن أيوب) was the first Sultan of Egypt and Syria, and led the Muslim opposition to the Crusaders, recapturing Palestine after 88 years of Crusader rule. Respected by his adversaries, including English monarch Richard the Lionheart, Saladin was known for his noble and chivalrous behavior.

Saladin

Record Holders

Adam Rainer (1889 — March 4, 1950)

Adam Rainer is the only person in recorded history to have been both a dwarf and a giant. At the age of 18, he was four feet tall, then a sudden growth spurt (possibly the byproduct of a pituitary tumor) took him to a height of over seven feet. He was bedridden for the rest of his life.

Sports

Jack Taylor (January 14, 1874 — March 4, 1938)

Chicago Cubs pitcher Jack Taylor holds the MLB record for pitching in 187 consecutive complete games from 1901 to 1906.

The month of March, from the illuminated manuscript
Les Très Riches Heures du duc de Berry

March: The Story of a Month

The Third Month

In ancient Rome, March was the first month of the year. As the first month of spring, in the Mediterranean climate it marked the beginning of the military campaign season. That's why March (Martius) is named in honor of Mars, the Roman god of war.

Although the first month of the year was moved back to January sometime during the transition of Rome from a kingdom to a republic (historians differ), March was the first month of the year in Russia until the end of the 15th Century, and is the first month of the year in many other cultures and religions.

In the northern hemisphere, March 1 marks the beginning of meteorological spring. In the southern hemisphere, March is the equivalent of September, making southern hemisphere March the beginning of autumn.

March is one of the seven months that have 31 days in it. March starts on the same day of the week as November every year, and except for leap years starts on the same day as February. March starts on the same day of the week as the previous June except for leap years, and in leap years starts on the same day as the previous September and December.

March in Other Cultures

In Finland, March is called *maaliskuu* (earthy month). In Ukraine, it's *березень* (birch tree). Other names for March include *Lentmona*t (Saxon), *Hyld-monath* (Angles), and *sušec* (Slovene).

March Symbols

Birthstones: Aquamarine and bloodstone, both representing courage.

Aquamarine

Birth Flowers
Daffodils

Daffodils in Bagatelle Park, Paris, France

March Events

Honorary months: Presidents, Congresses, and nations around the world issue proclamations recognizing particular months to honor certain causes. These events generally fall in March. (All US unless otherwise noted.)

- National Nutrition Month

- American Red Cross Month

- Women's History Month (celebrated in Canada during October)

- Irish-American Heritage Month

- Colorectal Cancer Awareness Month

- Fire Prevention Month (The Philippines)

Women's Suffrage picket line, 1917

"March Madness": (United States) The NCAA Men's Division I Basketball Championship, popularly known as "March Madness" or the "Big Dance," is a single-elimination tournament to establish the champion college basketball team.

Multi-day events: Some March events span multiple days.

- **Nineteen Day Fast:** (Bahá'í Faith) March 2 through March 20

Movable events: Some events change dates from year to year.

- **Mardi Gras:** French for "Fat Tuesday," this celebration takes place the day before Ash Wednesday, the beginning of the Lenten season. The New Orleans Mardi Gras celebration is perhaps the most famous, but Mardi Gras and the Carnival season (between Ephiphany and Ash Wednesday) are celebrated in many areas with large Catholic populations. Mardi Gras can take place anywhere from February 3 to March 9 in regular years, and from February 4 to March 9 in leap years.

- **Casimir Pulaski Day:** (Illinois) The first Monday in March is observed as a holiday in Illinois, in memory of the Revolutionary War cavalry officer born in Poland. Dates range from March 1 to March 7.

Mardi Gras Night Parade, New Orleans, 2012

March Zodiac Signs

From the perspective of someone on Earth, the Sun appears to move through the sky throughout the year, along a path astronomers call the ecliptic plane. The ecliptic plane is divided into twelve constellations, known as the zodiac, based on traditionally observed patterns of stars. On your birthday, you can't see your constellation, because it's part of the daytime sky.

The zodiac was first developed by Babylonian astronomers about 2,500 years ago. Because they were unaware that the Earth wobbles like a spinning top (a motion known as *precession*), they didn't make allowance for the fact that the Sun's path through the zodiac changes over time.

That means there are now two sets of dates for your birth sign. The *tropical dates* are the original Babylonian dates; the *siderial dates* tell you where the Sun actually appears as it moves along its annual path.

Zodiac signs in March are Aquarius and Pisces.

Aquarius

Tropical January 20 to February 19

Siderial February 12 to March 8 (March 9 in leap years)

Aquarius is one of the oldest recognized constellations, originally representing the Babylonian god Ea. In Latin, Aquarius means "water-carrier," represented in its symbol. In Greek mythology, Aquarius is sometimes associated with Deucalion, who survived a world-cleansing flood. In Chinese astronomy, it is known as the Black Tortoise of the North (北方玄武, Běi Fāng Xuán Wǔ).

In astrology, Aquarius is considered to be masculine and extroverted, and despite the name is an air sign. Aquarians are supposed to be philanthropical, inventive, and individualistic.

Pisces

Tropical February 20 to March 20

Siderial March 15 to April 14

In the Roman legend of Venus and her son Cupid, they escaped the clutches of Typhon, known as the "father of all monsters," by transforming into fish and tying themselves together with rope. That's why the name Pisces is plural for fish. The constellation appears as a somewhat ragged "V" shape, representing the rope, with the "fish" located at the two rope ends.

In astrology, Pisces is a water sign, compatible with the other water signs Cancer and Scorpio, as well as with the earth signs Taurus, Virgo, and Capricorn. Pisceans are supposed to be imaginative, compassionate, unworldly, secretive, and escapist.

What Day of the Week?

On what day of the week does March 4 fall?

Unfortunately, this isn't an easy question. Because the calendar year is 365 days long (366 in leap years), it doesn't divide evenly by the seven days of the week.

Also, the Earth goes around the Sun in about 365-1/4 days, so a calendar tends to drift over time. That's why the same date falls on different weekdays in different years.

This is made even more complicated by a change in calendars that took place in 1582. Our modern calendar has its roots in ancient Rome, in a calendar reform conducted by Julius Caesar. Caesar commissioned mathematicians to attack the problem, and came up with the idea of *leap years*, and thus standardized the calendar for centuries to come. This was called the *Julian calendar.*

Over time, however, the small errors in Caesar's calculation compounded. That's why Pope Gregory XIII commissioned the *Gregorian calendar*, used in most of the world today. Some countries converted in 1582, when the calendar was first developed; some converted later; other still haven't changed.

Gregorian and Julian aren't the only types of calendars. The Hebrew year, the Islamic year, and many other calendars are used in different parts of the world and among different people.

You can convert Gregorian dates to other calendars, including the Hebrew calendar, the Islamic calendar, and even the Mayan calendar by visiting the Fourmilab Calendar Converter at http://www.fourmilab.ch/documents/calendar/.

A 50-year brass perpetual calendar.

Copyright, Credit, and Contact

Follow Us

Our blog Dobson's Improbable History features short articles on events and people associated with each day, and updates several times each week. Get the latest on Twitter @SidewiseThinker.

Sources and Art Credits

Primary research source is Wikipedia, supplemented by other sources and personal research. All art and photographs are from Wikimedia Commons unless otherwise identified, and are either in the public domain or used under a Creative Commons license. Attribution is provided where requested by the copyright owner or when of historical significance, listed below.

- The cover painting by Howard Chandler Christy, "Scene at the Signing of the Constitution of the United States," is in the public domain. The original painting, created in 1940, currently hangs in the US House of Representatives.

- The photograph of the Preamble to the US Constitution is in the public domain.

- The photograph of the Kaziuko mugė fair is in the public domain.

- The flag of the Confederate States of America is in the public domain.

- The photograph of the Forth Bridge is by Kim Traynor, and is licensed under the Creative Commons Attribution-Share Alike 3.0 Unported license.

- The US Navy photograph of the USS *Cyclops* is in the public domain.

- The publicity photographs of Paula Prentiss and Barbara McNair are in the public domain.

- The movie poster for *The Perils of Pauline* is in the public domain because its copyright has expired.

- The photograph of Ed "Big Daddy" Roth's 1961 custom car "Beatnik Bandit" was taken by Nick Ares and is licensed under the Creative Commons Attribution-Share Alike 2.0 Generic license.

- The 1901 photograph of the Houdini brothers is in the public domain because its copyright has expired.

- The 1723 caricature of Antonio Vivaldi by Pier Leone Ghezzi is in the public domain because its copyright has expired.

- The 15th century portrait of Henry the Navigator is by Nuno Gonçalves and is in the public domain.

- The 1933 Goudey baseball card of Dazzy Vance is in the public domain because its copyright was not renewed.

- The 1910 photograph of Sam Langford is from the George Grantham Bain Collection of the Library of Congress Prints and Photographs Division and is in the public domain because its copyright has expired.

- The publicity photograph of Minnie Pearl is in the public domain.

- The daguerrotype of Nikolai Gogol was taken in 1845 by Sergey Levitsky, and is in the public domain.

- The photograph of Commodore Matthew C. Perry was taken by Mathew Brady and is in the public domain.

- The portrait of Saladin is by Cristofano dell'Altissimo and was painted sometime before 1568. The photograph is by Saliko, and is licensed under the Creative Commons Attribution-Share Alike 3.0 Unported license.

- The illustration of the month of March is from the French Gothic illuminated manuscript *Les Très Riches Heures du duc de Berry* by the Limbourg Brothers, Jean Colombe, and an intermediate painter whose name is lost to history.

- The photograph of aquamarine has been released into the public domain.